IMAGES
of America

SANTA FE
A HISTORICAL WALKING TOUR

IMAGES
of America

SANTA FE
A HISTORICAL WALKING TOUR

Jon Hunner, Shirley Lail, Pedro Domínguez, Darren Court, and
Lucinda Silva

ARCADIA

Published by Arcadia Publishing,
an imprint of Tempus Publishing, Inc.
3047 N. Lincoln Ave., Suite 410
Chicago, IL 60657

Printed in Great Britain.

Library of Congress Catalog Card Number: 00-107737

For all general information contact Arcadia Publishing at:
Telephone 843-853-2070
Fax 843-853-0044
E-Mail sales@arcadiapublishing.com

For customer service and orders:
Toll-Free 1-888-313-2665

Visit us on the internet at http://www.arcadiapublishing.com

WOMAN WALKING ALONG SAN FRANCISCO STREET, 1918. A smartly dressed woman crosses the corner of San Francisco Street and Don Gaspar Avenue. The horse and buggy was still in use, but it was being phased out by the "horseless carriage." (Courtesy of MNM, #14,142.)

CONTENTS

ACKNOWLEDGMENTS

Santa Fe: A Historical Walking Tour is a collaborative effort of many people. Darren Court, Pedro Domínguez, Shirley Lail, and Lucinda Silva, graduate students in the Public History Program at New Mexico State University (NMSU), devoted many hours to researching, writing, and laying out the book. Shirley and Brian Lail also took the contemporary images of the buildings. The historic photographs come from three archives in New Mexico. We would like to thank Arthur Olívas and Richard Rudisill at the Museum of New Mexico Photo Archives in Santa Fe for allowing us to use their images, and for their able assistance. Sandra Jaramillo and Shan Sutton at the New Mexico State Records and Archives Center in Santa Fe also deserve our gratitude for their assistance and permission to publish the photographs from their collection. At the Rio Grande Historical Collection at the New Mexico State University Library, we would like to thank Austin Hoover and Dennis Daily for uncovering the rare historic photographs they hold and allowing us to use them. Thanks also go to our colleagues in the History Department at NMSU who have supported this project. Finally, we appreciate the help of Tom Rakness, our editor at Arcadia Publishing.

Since the Public History Program at NMSU receives part of the profit from the sale of *Santa Fe: A Historical Walking Tour*, we would like to thank you for purchasing this book. If you would like more information about the program, please visit our web site at:
http://web.nmsu.edu/~publhist.

INTRODUCTION

Santa Fe: A Historical Walking Tour explores the four hundred years of history of the "City Different" in a unique way. First, it is a history of the oldest capital city in the United States. Second, it is a guide to a walking tour of the historic downtown district. And third, it examines the evolution of Santa Fe's architectural designs. This book explores the changes in the urban landscape of Santa Fe by showing historic and contemporary photographs of many of the most important buildings in the city. By tracing the transformation of these buildings over the last 150 years, one will see how the architectural canvas of Santa Fe changed styles in the last half of the 1800s, and then returned to its Native American and Spanish colonial roots in the 20th century. Walking along the tour route, the reader can trace these changes, as well as enjoy the rich history and heritage of Santa Fe.

Santa Fe has undergone numerous transformations over the centuries. Spanish colonization in New Mexico began in 1598, when Don Juan de Oñate led a group of settlers from Mexico to a site 30 miles north of present-day Santa Fe. In 1610 (around the same time that the English established Jamestown), Don Pedro de Peralta replaced Oñate as governor and moved the capital to its present location along the banks of the Santa Fe River. *La Villa Real de Santa Fe de St. Francis de Assisi,* or the "Royal City of the Holy Faith of St. Francis of Assisi," was one of the most remote outposts of the Spanish Empire and an isolated capital on the far northern frontier of New Spain. For centuries, Santa Fe was a small village, neglected and ignored, but from the beginning it has been a diverse community. Spaniards and Mexican immigrants, local Native Americans, and *mestizos* (people of mixed heritage) have lived next to each other, married, raised families, and at times fought one another in the houses and streets of Santa Fe.

Santa Fe has seen a variety of rulers over its history. From 1610 to 1680, Spain controlled Santa Fe. The Pueblo Revolt of 1680, the most successful attempt by Native Americans to expel European settlers in North American history, forced the Spanish and their allies to flee 300 miles south, and leaders from the pueblos held court in the Palace of the Governors. In 1692, Don Diego de Vargas reconquered New Mexico and reestablished Spanish rule, until Mexico gained its independence in 1821. From 1821 to the Mexican-American War in 1846, New Mexico was the most populated of the northern states of independent Mexico. New

Mexico became a territory of the United States in 1850, but the Confederate flag flew over the Plaza in 1862. In 1912, New Mexico won statehood and became the 47th state in the union. Santa Fe's four hundred years of existence have produced a rich history that will be highlighted as one looks at the archival photographs of *Santa Fe: A Historical Walking Tour*.

As a historically diverse town, Santa Fe's architectural styles reflect the rich cultures of its inhabitants. Throughout the centuries, new immigrants from Spain, Mexico, and the United States added their architectural traditions and building methods to the existing styles, and as a result, transformed how Santa Fe looked. The predominant architectural style of Santa Fe from 1610 to the 1850s grew out of the Spanish and Moorish designs and technology, which combined with Native American building methods. The Moors introduced mud-dried adobe bricks into Spain, which the Spaniards brought to the New World. Now called the Pueblo Spanish Style, during colonial times it was merely how ordinary people built their homes. Private homes were constructed with little thought to creating a coherent style. The thick abode walls provided insulation against the winter cold and summer heat, the hefty pine *vigas* (roof beams) supported the ceilings, and mud stucco was the only material available to cover exterior walls. This vernacular style, seen in the flat roofs, thick adobe walls, rounded corners, exposed *vigas*, and brown stucco, emerged because most Native American and Hispanic residents used the same tools and materials as their neighbors, and used construction methods passed down from their ancestors.

After the United States annexed New Mexico in 1846, a new look, the Territorial Style, quickly swept the region. Combining adobe materials with the Greek Revival architecture popular on the East Coast at the time, the Territorial Style used white, triangular pediments over windows and doors, square, white porch posts, and a brick parapet which topped the adobe walls. The Territorial Style dominated until the Atchison, Topeka, and Santa Fe Railroad arrived in Santa Fe in 1881. With new building materials like tin roofing panels and kiln-fired bricks, combined with popular Victorian architectural styles such as Second Empire, Queen Anne, and Gothic Revival, Santa Fe's new homes and public buildings underwent a dramatic transformation. Archbishop Jean Lamy helped introduce such styles when he commissioned St. Francis Cathedral and Loretto Chapel. Adobes were no longer the building material of choice for the "City Different." In 1889 alone, more than 3.5 million bricks arrived in Santa Fe by rail to supply the construction demands of that year. After centuries of an urban landscape built of adobe bricks and looking like a Native American pueblo, downtown Santa Fe, with its new Victorian structures, began looking like many small cities in "Gilded Age America."

Santa Fe city officials and boosters used New Mexico's statehood in 1912 to reinvent the city. As you will see in the following photographs, many of the city's historic buildings were close to collapse and in need of serious renewal. Influenced by the nation's "City Beautiful" movement and Germany's historic preservation movement, city booster Harry Dorman wrote: "The City of Santa Fe is planning extensive improvements that include the laying out of streets, the restriction of manufacturing plants to a suitable district. . . and the bringing about of some sort of architectural homogeneity." Unlike most "City Beautiful" plans, Santa Fe's architectural style was not Beaux Arts classicism, but the Pueblo Spanish Style. Commenting on the 1912 city plan, historian Chris Wilson recently observed: "Architectural image became central to stimulating tourism and reversing economic decline. Soon the chamber of commerce was promoting Santa Fe not as another 'City Beautiful' but as the 'City Different.'" Santa Fe once again negotiated its heritage, transforming itself into a city different from other American cities, and also a city different from its recent Victorian past.

The return of Santa Fe to its architectural roots quickly received official approval. Around 1910, the Palace of the Governors (the seat of government from 1610 to 1885) was restored from its Victorian Style back to its original Pueblo Spanish appearance. Thus began the Pueblo Spanish Style movement, which some call the "Spanish Pueblo Revival." Since no coherent Pueblo Spanish Style existed before 1850, the creation of this style in the 20th century is not a revival, but a new regional architectural movement. Along with Territorial Revival, the Pueblo

Spanish Style has dominated both public and private construction for almost one hundred years. To protect the architectural legacy of the "City Different," Santa Fe instituted statutes in 1957 to enforce the homogenous Santa Fe Style. The law created the Historic Design Review Board, which even today evaluates new construction and scrutinizes any changes to existing structures and signage within the historic districts to insure that Santa Fe preserves its Pueblo Spanish and Territorial look. So, the final goal of *Santa Fe: A Historical Walking Tour* is to illustrate the changes in the urban landscape of the "City Different" and describe the return to its Pueblo, Spanish, and Territorial roots. At the beginning of the 20th century, Santa Fe was losing its historic structures to neglect and progress. The invention of the Pueblo Spanish Style invigorated the historic preservation community and laid a foundation for preservation efforts for the next century. Looking at the photographs and captions of the buildings in this book and walking the tour, you will gain a new understanding of the "City Different" and the historical forces that have made it a unique community.

The chapters of *Santa Fe: A Historical Walking Tour* are organized geographically. The first chapter focuses on the Plaza itself and the four streets which surround the Plaza. Chapter Two begins at the southeast corner of the Plaza and goes south along the Old Santa Fe Trail to San Miguel Mission, and then explores the area to the east of the Plaza. Chapter Three starts at the northeast corner of the Plaza and wanders through the north, west, and southwest parts of the downtown districts. Although this book is intended to serve as a walking tour, some of the sites, like Rosario Hill and the train station, might be too far away from the Plaza for some walkers. A figure number, title, contemporary address in parentheses, and year that the photograph was taken identify each image.

In the credit for each photograph, we use the following abbreviations: **MNM** for the **Museum of New Mexico Photo Archives; NMSRAC-DOD** for the **New Mexico State Records Archive Center's Department of Development collection; RGHC-NMSU** for the **Rio Grande Historical Collection;** and **Lail** for **Shirley and Brian Lail's images.** The photographer is credited when known.

Walking Tour of Santa Fe

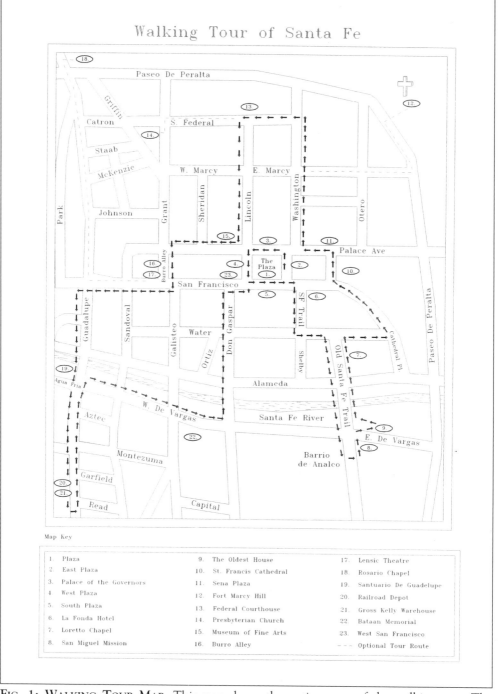

Map Key

1.	Plaza	9.	The Oldest House
2.	East Plaza	10.	St. Francis Cathedral
3.	Palace of the Governors	11.	Sena Plaza
4.	West Plaza	12.	Fort Marcy Hill
5.	South Plaza	13.	Federal Courthouse
6.	La Fonda Hotel	14.	Presbyterian Church
7.	Loretto Chapel	15.	Museum of Fine Arts
8.	San Miguel Mission	16.	Burro Alley

17.	Lensic Theatre
18.	Rosario Chapel
19.	Santuario De Guadelupe
20.	Railroad Depot
21.	Gross Kelly Warehouse
22.	Bataan Memorial
23.	West San Francisco
- - -	Optional Tour Route

FIG. 1: WALKING TOUR MAP. This map shows the entire route of the walking tour. The general areas of interest are shown here. At the beginning of every chapter, a map of that area of Santa Fe will show the location of each building and photograph.

One

THE PLAZA

FIG. 1.1: THE PLAZA, 1861. The Elsberg-Amberg wagon train stopped in front of the Palace of the Governors in 1861, in one of the earliest photographs of the Plaza. Having traveled 900 miles along the Santa Fe Trail from Kansas City to the "City Different," such wagon trains found profit and pleasure at the end of the trail. (Courtesy of MNM, #11,254.)

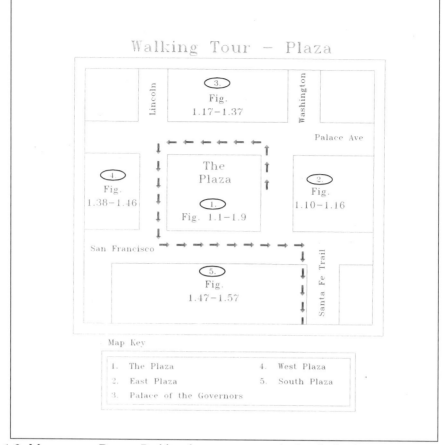

FIG. 1.2: MAP OF THE PLAZA. Building locations are marked with the figure number given to each photograph. For example, Figure 1.17 is the first photograph of the Palace of the Governors. (Map by S. Lail.)

FIG. 1.3: THE PLAZA, 1869. The Plaza, an integral part of the town since its founding in 1610, begins to show the influence of the United States right after the Civil War. The picket fence and the newly erected Memorial to the Soldiers at the center left changed the Plaza's appearance from a Hispanic plaza to an Anglicized town square. Looking east across the Plaza, La Parroquia, the main church that served the downtown area, can be seen center right. (Courtesy of MNM, #11,252 by N. Brown.)

FIG 1.4: THE PLAZA, c. 1870s. Burros tied to the Plaza's picket fence await their owner's return. Burros, brought to New Mexico by the Spanish, were a common sight in Santa Fe, as they carried firewood and trade goods. The Soldier's Memorial and the Palace of the Governors are in the background. (Courtesy of NMSRAC-DOD, Box 53, #2,291.)

FIG. 1.5: THE PLAZA, 1880. The Ninth Cavalry Band entertained Santa Feans from the Plaza's gazebo, possibly on July 4th, 1880. The Ninth Cavalry, one of the famous Buffalo Soldiers units of the U.S. Army comprised of African Americans, fought in the Indian Wars in the Southwest in the 1870s and 1880s. (Courtesy of MNM, #50,887 by B. Wittick.)

FIG. 1.6: THE PLAZA, 1890–91. Throughout the town's history, Santa Feans have enjoyed meeting their neighbors on the Plaza's benches. The Exchange Hotel is seen in the distance between the gazebo and the monument. (Courtesy of MNM, #11,283 by W.E. Hook.)

FIG. 1.7: THE PLAZA, 2000. The Memorial to the Soldiers at the center of the Plaza towers over residents and tourists who bask in the afternoon sun like their predecessors in Fig. 1.6. (Photo by Lail.)

FIG. 1.8: THE PLAZA, c. 1940s. Looking from the southwest corner of the Plaza at San Francisco Street and Lincoln Avenue, the Plaza appears abandoned in this spring snowstorm. (Courtesy of NMSRAC-DOD, Box 48, #1,465.)

FIG. 1.9: THE PLAZA, EARLY 1900s. As the center of Santa Fe, the Plaza was a magnet for fashionably dressed Santa Feans out for a stroll. (Courtesy of MNM, #11,299.)

FIG 1.10: EAST PLAZA, 1866. In the 1700s, the Plaza covered a larger area than today. It extended from its present location east to La Parroquia, the parish church with the two towers on the upper right. The one-story adobe buildings seen here bordering the east side of the plaza were built in the 1800s. (Courtesy of MNM, #38,025 by N. Brown.)

FIG 1.11: CATRON BLOCK (53 OLD SANTA FE TRAIL), 1915. Thomas Catron, a Union veteran of the Civil War, came to New Mexico in 1866 to make his fortune. With the help of Stephen Elkins, Catron started the infamous Santa Fe Ring. This corrupt political group dominated business and land deals throughout New Mexico into the 1900s. This Italianate-style building, built in 1891, was the site of the Catron & Elkins law firm, and shows how Victorian styles transformed the look of downtown Santa Fe. (Courtesy of MNM, #67,593 by E.V. Harris.)

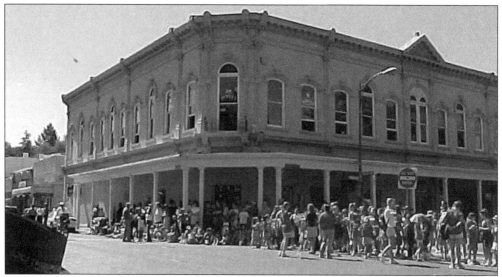

FIG 1.12: CATRON BLOCK, 2000. The Catron Block, at the northeast corner of the Plaza, has seen many tenants and parades over the last century. (Photo by Lail.)

FIG 1.13: EAST PLAZA, c. 1950. In 1881, the newly arrived railroad brought a flood of immigrants to New Mexico, along with their East Coast culture and architectural styles. The First National Bank building (center left) was built in 1912. The Neo-Classical building, with its white Grecian columns, was a sharp contrast to the nearby adobe structures. (Courtesy of NMSRAC-DOD, Box 48, #1,463.)

FIG 1.14: EAST PLAZA, 2000. Eventually the Catron Building was remodeled and gained a portal, or covered sidewalk. The front of the First National Bank, shown in the above photo, was replaced with a Pueblo Spanish facade. (Photo by Lail.)

FIG 1.15: EAST PLAZA, c. 1950. The wide variety of Victorian architectural styles that came to Santa Fe in the late 1800s and early 1900s changed the look of the city. By the 1910s, a shift back to Pueblo Spanish and Territorial Styles began to establish a homogenous look, and the Santa Fe Style was born. Buildings, such as the First National Bank in the center of the photo, eventually were remodeled to match the new Santa Fe Style. (Courtesy of NMSRAC-DOD, Box 48, #1,494.)

FIG 1.16: EAST PLAZA, c. 1920. Looking west on Palace Avenue, the north side of the Catron Building is on the left. The Palace of the Governors is in the center of the photograph. Although Santa Fe acquired streetlights in 1891, and street signs in 1900, almost all of the streets in the city were packed dirt until the 1920s. (Courtesy of MNM, #163,829 by W.H. Roberts.)

FIG. 1.17: PALACE OF THE GOVERNORS, EL PALACIO (105 WEST PALACE) BEFORE 1885.
Looking northeast across the Plaza, one sees the south side of the Palace of the Governors as it looked for centuries. *El Palacio* was the seat of government for New Mexico from 1610 to 1885. Spanish colonial, Mexican, and U.S. Territorial governors, as well as Confederate and Union generals during the Civil War, all resided here. (Courtesy of NMSRAC-DOD, Box 48, #1,467.)

FIG. 1.18: PALACE OF THE GOVERNORS, 1903. After New Mexico became a U.S. territory in 1846, a gradual but dramatic political, economic, and cultural change occurred. In the 1880s, *El Palacio* was remodeled to reflect the Victorian architectural fashion popular at the time. Compared to Fig. 1.17, the portal has an ornate railing on top and square posts. Also notice the newly installed telegraph poles. (Courtesy of RGHC-NMSU, Foster Collection, Ms 264.6 by C.A. Kaadt.)

FIG. 1.19: PALACE OF THE GOVERNORS. Looking west at the Governor's Palace, the Victorian renovation of the 1880s is clearly seen. After the territorial legislature moved to the new capital in 1885, lawyers and other businesses rented space in the building. (Courtesy of RGHC-NMSU, Branigan Library Collection, #A76–157–169.)

FIG. 1.20: PALACE OF THE GOVERNORS, 1911. With patriotic bunting hanging from the portal, residents recreate the 1692 re-conquest of Santa Fe by Don Diego de Vargas. In addition to the conquistador re-enactors on horseback in front of the portal, Native Americans gather around a cross on the right. (Courtesy of MNM, #117,757 by Jesse Nusbaum.)

FIG. 1.21: PALACE OF THE GOVERNORS' COURTYARD, JULY 1911. Celebrants in the annual de Vargas pageant assemble in the courtyard of the Palace before their *entrada* onto the Plaza. St. Francis Cathedral rises in the background. (Courtesy of MNM, #155,675.)

FIG. 1.22: PALACE OF THE GOVERNORS' COURTYARD, JULY 1911. The honor guard for the Diego de Vargas parade illustrates the preservation of Hispanic heritage in Santa Fe. The pageant, now held in September, continues to celebrate the re-conquest of New Mexico by de Vargas in 1692. (Courtesy of MNM, #118,255 by Jesse Nusbaum.)

FIG. 1.23: PALACE OF THE GOVERNORS, 1912. Native Americans join in the de Vargas pageant. Despite the pageant celebrating the re-conquest of New Mexico by de Vargas after the Pueblo Revolt of 1680, many Native Americans participated in the fiesta until recently. (Courtesy of MNM, #22,614 by Jesse Nusbaum.)

FIG. 1.24: PALACE OF THE GOVERNORS, c. 1920s. A traditional dance performed on a stage in front of the Palace shows the ceremonial costumes of the local Puebloans and two drummers in white shirts. Also notice the *kiva* ladder on the right, brought to the Plaza for the ceremony. (Courtesy of RGHC-NMSU, Ms 186 Box 27, File 7, #01860356 by W. Bynner.)

FIG. 1.25: PALACE OF THE GOVERNORS, c. 1920s. A Native American Deer Dance is performed in front of *El Palacio*. The bent-over dancers in the white shirts holding sticks in their hands represent deer coming down from the hills. (Courtesy of RGHC-NMSU, Ms 186 box 43, folder 4, #01862004 by W. Bynner.)

FIG. 1.26: PALACE OF THE GOVERNORS, c. 1920s. This ceremony possibly re-enacted one of the first meetings between Native Americans, a Spanish Father Marcos, and Estevan, a Moorish slave in 1539. (Courtesy of RGHC-NMSU, Ms 186 box 43, folder 4, #01862005 by W. Bynner.)

FIG. 1.27: PALACE OF THE GOVERNORS, 1917. In the 1910s, after the State of New Mexico established the Museum of New Mexico and gave the Palace to the museum, the building once again was transformed, this time back to its original style. Exposed *vigas* (roof beams) sticking out from the rounded parapet replaced the ornate railings. Massive tree trunks supplanted the square posts which supported the portal. This remodeling of the Palace was one of the first attempts to recreate a distinctively Santa Fe architectural look—the Pueblo Spanish Style. (Courtesy of MNM, #11,281.)

FIG. 1.28: PALACE OF THE GOVERNORS, 1924. After its transformation into the Museum of New Mexico in 1909, the Palace continued to be a focal point of the Plaza. Notice the large tree trunks which supported the portal roof and the scrolled corbels that topped them. (Courtesy of MNM, #10,598 by T.H. Parkhurst.)

FIG. 1.29: PALACE OF THE GOVERNORS. Many historic events have occurred under the portal of *El Palacio*. In 1680, Native Americans revolted throughout New Mexico, and Spanish settlers sought refuge behind the walls of the Palace. Governor Otermin and his soldiers fought the rebels from this portal, but eventually retreated to El Paso del Norte, 300 miles to the south. From 1680 until the re-conquest in 1692, Native Americans lived in the Palace and added a second floor. (Courtesy of NMSRAC DOD, Box 48, #1,413.)

FIG. 1.30: PALACE OF THE GOVERNORS' PORTAL, 1935. Pueblo Indians have sold jewelry and crafts under the portal for decades. The arts and crafts are made by family members and must pass a rigorous examination to ensure the authenticity of the merchandise. (Courtesy of MNM, #6,852 by T. Harmon Parkhurst.)

FIG. 1.31: PALACE OF THE GOVERNORS, 1928. The Pasatiempo Parade passes in front of the Palace to the delight of thousands. Created in 1924 by several members of the art colony in Santa Fe, this parade illustrates how Santa Feans, even in the 1920s, celebrated their eccentricities. (Courtesy of MNM, #132,200.)

Fig. 1.32: Palace of the Governors, c. 1940s. During World War II, young men were inducted into the Armed Forces in front of the Palace. (Courtesy of NMSRAC-DOD, Box 48, #55,565.)

Fig. 1.33: Palace of the Governors, c. 1940s. In addition to induction ceremonies, military parades also helped the war effort in Santa Fe. (Courtesy of NMSRAC-DOD, Box 48, #1,447.)

FIG. 1.34: PALACE OF THE GOVERNORS, c. 1940S. Looking west at *El Palacio* from the corner of Palace Avenue and Washington Street. (Courtesy of NMSRAC-DOD, Box 48, #1,461.)

FIG. 1.35: PALACE OF THE GOVERNORS, 2000. The oldest governmental building in the United States, the Palace of the Governors reigns supreme on the Plaza. (Photo by Lail.)

FIG. 1.36: PALACE OF THE GOVERNORS, c. 1940S. Looking northeast at the Palace from Lincoln Avenue. (Courtesy of NMSRAC-DOD, Box 48, #1,462.)

FIG. 1.37: PALACE OF THE GOVERNORS, 2000. *El Palacio* continues to attract tourists to the Palace of the Governors' Museum and portal. (Photo by Lail.)

FIG. 1.38: THE PLAZA LOOKING WEST TOWARD LINCOLN AVENUE, 1866. The west side of the plaza right after the Civil War had residences and businesses in the one and two-story adobe structures. (Courtesy of MNM, #11,256.)

FIG. 1.39 THE PLAZA, 1866. This is a view of the Plaza looking west. The gazebo in the center part of the Plaza seen in Fig. 1.38 was moved to the north side of the Plaza, and the Soldiers' Memorial was erected in 1866. (Courtesy of MNM, #23,136.)

FIG. 1.40: WEST SIDE OF THE PLAZA AT LINCOLN AVENUE, 1866. These adobe buildings with flat roofs and wooden, square columns are typical of the Territorial Style of architecture, which came to New Mexico after the Mexican-American War in 1846. (Courtesy of MNM, #11,177.)

Fig. 1.41: Lincoln Avenue at the Plaza Looking North, c. 1900. By the end of the 1880s, the west side of the Plaza was filled up with two-story Territorial-style buildings. Note the telegraph poles. At the far end of Lincoln Avenue, the pitched roof of the Federal Courthouse is seen. (Courtesy of MNM, #14,120.)

Fig. 1.42: Southwest Corner of the Plaza, 1915. From this corner is a good view of two drugstores that were institutions in Santa Fe. To the right is Zook's Pharmacy, and across the street is Fischer's Drug Company. The sign facing the street between the columns reads: "Welcome to the Capital." (Courtesy of MNM, #11,332 by Jesse L. Nusbaum.)

FIG. 1.43: LINCOLN AVENUE AT THE PLAZA, 1918. Looking south along the west side of the Plaza towards San Francisco Street shows the dramatic transformation that occurred after the turn of the 20th century. The three-story brick building on the right was at one time a grocery store and a barbershop. When it burned down, a Pueblo Spanish Style structure took its place. (Courtesy of MNM, #14,123.)

FIG. 1.44: SOUTHWEST CORNER OF THE PLAZA AT SAN FRANCISCO STREET AND LINCOLN AVENUE, 2000. The building at this corner was a Territorial Style from 1850s to 1910s. Then a three-story Victorian style structure replaced it. Now a Territorial Revival building stands at the corner, showing how the cultural landscape of Santa Fe has returned to its pre-Gilded Age roots. (Photo by Lail.)

FIG. 1.45: CORNER OF LINCOLN AVENUE AT PALACE AVENUE, 1917. A fire gutted the Monarch Cash Grocery on December 19, 1917, and caved in the ceiling. A Pueblo Spanish-style movie theater replaced it. Unlike today, with the Plaza district full of galleries and stores catering to tourists, until the 1970s Santa Feans often came to the Plaza to do their everyday shopping. (Courtesy of MNM, #14,093.)

FIG. 1.46: WEST SIDE OF PLAZA, 1928. After a fire destroyed the Monarch Cash Grocery, a Pueblo Spanish-style movie theater rose at the corner of Lincoln and Palace Avenues. The two towers of this building mirrored the Fine Arts Museum across the street. (Courtesy of MNM, #91,160.)

Fig. 1.47: San Francisco Street at the Plaza, 1868. People busily tended their wagons along San Francisco Street. Santa Fe Trail traders would joyously arrive at the Plaza after three months of hard travel from Kansas City. Missourian William Becknell opened the Santa Fe Trail in 1821, and the railroad effectively closed it in 1881. In the far background is La Parroquia, the main downtown church, built in the early 1700s. (Courtesy of MNM, #70,437 by Nicholas Brown.)

FIG. 1.48: SAN FRANCISCO STREET AT THE PLAZA, 1868. Pictured are Santa Fe Trail wagon trains loading and unloading merchandise. These wagons often transported 5,000 pounds of goods 900 miles from Kansas City, Missouri, to Santa Fe. During the 1800s, merchants used the buildings on the south side of the Plaza as stores and warehouses for their wares. (Courtesy of MNM, #11,329.)

FIG. 1.49: SAN FRANCISCO STREET AT LINCOLN AVENUE, 1897–1898. By the turn of the century, telephone poles lined San Francisco Street. Looming in the background, St. Francis Cathedral (which replaced La Parroquia) shows the shift to Victorian architectural styles. Because of the Santa Fe Trail merchants who opened stores along the south side of the Plaza, this block evolved into the retail center of the town with restaurants, hotels, and shops. (Courtesy of MNM, #124,334 by John B. Reall.)

FIG. 1.50: SAN FRANCISCO STREET AT LINCOLN AVENUE, 2000. A homogenous facade of Santa Fe Style now lines San Francisco Street at the Plaza. (Photo by Lail.)

FIG. 1.51: SAN FRANCISCO STREET, c. 1920s. Along San Francisco Street, parked cars from the 1920s show the incredible change from horse to automobile, which occurred in the early 1900s. Just to the left above the trees can be seen St. Francis Cathedral. (Courtesy of MNM, #135,013.)

FIG. 1.52: SAN FRANCISCO STREET AT PLAZA, c. 1940–1943. A lot has changed since the days of the Santa Fe Trail. The architecture has shifted from the adobe structure to Italianate style, though some buildings still retain their Pueblo Spanish look. Also new to the Plaza are the signs advertising everything from Coca-Cola to bars and billiards. A passerby could also stop in and watch the art of blanket weaving at Julius Gans' Southwest Arts and Crafts. (Courtesy of MNM, #10,639.)

FIG. 1.53: DE VARGAS PARADE ALONG SAN FRANCISCO STREET, 1911. On September 16, 1712, Captain General Juan Paez Hurtado gave an order for a fiesta to be held every year as a reminder of the re-conquest of New Mexico by Don Diego de Vargas over the Pueblo Indians. The Fiesta de Santa Fe continues the tradition every September with religious observances, parades, and celebrations. (Courtesy of MNM, #52,748.)

FIG. 1.54: CORNER OF SAN FRANCISCO STREET AND OLD SANTA FE TRAIL, 2000. Looking west along San Francisco Street, the old transportation block of the Santa Fe Trail traders now holds galleries, boutiques, and tourist stores. (Photo by Lail.)

Fig. 1.55: Z. Staab Building (118 West San Francisco Street), 1933–1934. The Staab Building was built in 1884, and by the 1930s, when the Charles Ilfeld Company resided there, was "wholesaler of everything." Notice the National Recovery Act eagle on the front door, signifying that the Ilfeld Company supported President Roosevelt's New Deal policies. (Courtesy of MNM, #10,778 by T. Harmon Parkhurst.)

FIG. 1.56: WOOLWORTH BUILDING (60 WEST SAN FRANCISCO STREET). The Woolworth Building, with its adobe walls and exposed *vigas*, was a landmark on the Plaza for locals and tourists. The store served the best Frito Pie in town. (Courtesy of NMSRAC-DOD, Box 48, #14,560.)

FIGURE 1.57: WOOLWORTH BUILDING, 2000. After decades on the Plaza, the F.W. Woolworth Co. closed its doors in the late 1990s. (Photo by Lail.)

Two

SOUTH AND EAST OF THE PLAZA

FIG. 2.1: EXCHANGE HOTEL AND THE SELIGMAN AND CLEVER STORE, (100 EAST SAN FRANCISCO STREET), 1855. One of the oldest photographs of Santa Fe looks southeast from the Plaza to the Exchange Hotel and the Seligman and Clever Store. The location of the hotel and store at the end of the Santa Fe Trail was undoubtedly beneficial. Sigmund Seligman and Charles P. Clever, both natives of Germany, became prominent promoters of the Santa Fe trade with the American communities on the Missouri River—trade which, more than any other factor, opened Santa Fe to the United States. Charles Clever also served as the Attorney General for the Territory of New Mexico during the Civil War. (Courtesy of MNM, #10,685.)

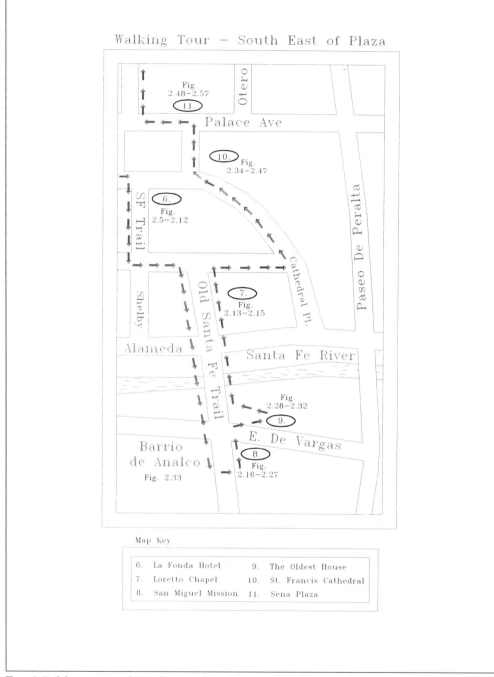

FIG. 2.2: MAP OF THE AREA SOUTH AND EAST OF THE PLAZA. Beginning at La Fonda Hotel across from the southeast corner of the Plaza, follow the arrows on the map. The figure numbers identify the photographs on the following pages. (Map by S. Lail.)

FIG. 2.3: EXCHANGE HOTEL, c. 1880S. The Exchange Hotel, located where La Fonda Hotel now stands, was Santa Fe's preeminent hotel during the latter part of the 19th century. In existence first as the U.S. Hotel, then the Exchange Hotel, the inn dated back at least to the time of the Mexican-American War (1846–1848). In 1871, an article in the Santa Fe *New Mexican* referred to the hotel as one of the finest in the West. (Courtesy of MNM, #39,368.)

FIG. 2.4: EXCHANGE HOTEL, 1900. At the dawn of the 20th century, the Exchange Hotel was in decline. The old hotel, now in disrepair, was a butcher shop. By 1919, the building was destroyed, as the City of Santa Fe began to recreate itself. (Courtesy of MNM, #105,576.)

FIG. 2.5: LA FONDA HOTEL, 1923. In 1919, the construction of La Fonda began—partly in response to the increasing importance of tourism and the Santa Fe mystique. With the sale of almost $200,000 in bonds, Santa Fe began building the new structure. The old Exchange Hotel was torn down, at least in part, by a World War I-era tank, with individual rides given to those purchasing the bonds. The new hotel was designed in the Pueblo Spanish style by the Rapp, Rapp, and Henderson architectural firm. (Courtesy of MNM, #40,752.)

FIG. 2.6: LA FONDA HOTEL, 1927. In 1927, La Fonda underwent a significant expansion to cater to the increasing number of tourists flocking to the "City Different." The recreation of the city as a mecca for those interested in the mystique of the West, Native American art and culture, and simply a more liberal atmosphere, was paying off. John Gaw Meem, an architect and historic preservationist, designed a six-story tower addition that looked like the mission bell towers at the pueblo of Acoma. His expansion, shown here on the far right during construction, almost doubled the size of the hotel. (Courtesy of MNM, #55,539, by Edward Kemp.)

FIG. 2.7: LA FONDA HOTEL, 1935. The most striking feature of the finished addition is the six-story bell tower shown here. The heavily buttressed walls, portal entrance at the rear, and exposed *vigas* (ceiling beams), all illustrate the fusion of Spanish and Native American cultures which produced the Santa Fe Style. (Courtesy of MNM, #10,690 by T. Harmon Parkhurst.)

FIG. 2.8: LA FONDA HOTEL, 1925. In response to the increasing commercialism and perceived elitism of the art community in Santa Fe, poet Witter Bynner and activist Dolly Sloan created the *Pasatiempo* in 1924. It was a free street festival open to the entire city, and the fiesta quickly

became one of the most popular in Santa Fe. Here, part of the parade passes by the open balconies of La Fonda. (Courtesy of MNM, #118,249 by T. Harmon Parkhurst.)

FIG. 2.9: LA FONDA HOTEL, c. 1920–1925. Soon after its opening, La Fonda was acquired by the Fred Harvey Company. The Harvey Company used La Fonda as a starting point for its popular "Indian Detour" tours. The lobby displayed a 15-square-foot Navajo sand painting and other Native American artifacts. The outside of the structure, with its Pueblo Spanish style also looked like a Native American pueblo. (Courtesy of MNM, #54,310 by T. Harmon Parkhurst.)

FIG. 2.10: LA FONDA HOTEL, 2000. La Fonda continues to rank as one of the best hotels in Santa Fe and has changed little since the 1920s, when its construction helped launch the Santa Fe style. (Photo by Lail.)

FIG. 2.11: LA FONDA HOTEL, 1935. This photograph aptly illustrates the architectural details of the Pueblo Spanish style, including the stepped stories, *canales* (rain spouts), corbel brackets, and the stucco finish. Also note the Curio Indian Shop in the front of the building, added in 1927. (Courtesy of MNM, #10,692 by T. Harmon Parkhurst.)

FIG. 2.12: LA FONDA HOTEL, 2000. Looking south from the Plaza down Old Santa Fe Trail, the distinct lines of La Fonda continue to evoke the architecture of a Native American pueblo. (Photo by Lail.)

FIG 2.13 : LORETTO CHAPEL (207 OLD SANTA FE TRAIL), 1874. In 1873, Bishop Lamy hired a French architect to build a Gothic Revival chapel for the Sisters of Loretto. The building was near completion when the young architect fell in love with the wife of Bishop Lamy's nephew. A quarrel resulted, and the architect was shot to death by the nephew while leaving a hotel room. The scandalous murder prevented the chapel from being completely finished. (Courtesy of MNM, #15,854.)

FIG 2.14: LORETTO CHAPEL, 2000. Exterior brown stucco covers the stonework to help incorporate the Gothic Revival chapel into the Pueblo Spanish style; however, the general design of the church was left unchanged. Along with St. Francis Cathedral, Loretto Chapel helped introduce Victorian architectural styles into Santa Fe. (Photo by Lail.)

FIG 2.15: LORETTO CHAPEL, 1935. This beautiful Gothic Revival chapel houses the world-famous Miraculous Staircase. After the murder of the Chapel's architect, Loretto Chapel was left without a staircase to the choir loft. The Sisters of Loretto decided to pray for a solution. A mysterious man answered the Sister's prayers by building a beautiful spiral staircase without a center support and using neither nails nor screws. (Courtesy of MNM, #51,395 by T.H. Parkhurst.)

FIG 2.16: SAN MIGUEL MISSION (401 OLD SANTA FE TRAIL), BEFORE 1872. Built after the founding of Santa Fe in 1610, San Miguel Mission is one of the oldest churches in the United States. The church was founded by Franciscan missionaries, and served primarily as a Catholic chapel for Indian servants. Archeological investigation beneath the church floor uncovered an earlier church foundation and potsherds dating Native American occupation to A.D. 1300. (Courtesy of RGHC-NMSU, Luther Foster Collection, Ms. 264.5 by C. Kaadt.)

FIG 2.17: SAN MIGUEL MISSION, c. 1870s. San Miguel has endured a turbulent history. Church officials were often at odds with the Spanish colonial government over whom would control the local Native Americans. In 1640, an angry Governor Rosas ordered the church closed. The conflict was eventually resolved, but San Miguel was torn down as a result of the conflict. The structure was rebuilt several years later, only to be burned in 1680 by rebelling Native Americans during the Pueblo Revolt. The church was again rebuilt in 1710. (Courtesy of NMSRAC-DOD, Box 48, #1,480 by C.A. Kaadt.)

FIG 2.18: SAN MIGUEL MISSION, 1940. At the turn of the 20th century, the inside of the Mission was redesigned to recreate a look as close to the original 17th century structure as possible. Customary wooden Stations of the Cross were added, as well as wooden pews and devotional carvings. The exterior of the Mission was not so faithfully reconstructed—the bell tower received a pitched roof and arched windows, different than the style seen in figure 2.16. (Courtesy of MNM, #103,527 by F. Fedor.)

FIG 2.19: SAN MIGUEL MISSION, 2000. In the 1950s, San Miguel underwent another restoration. The open bell tower replaced the pitched roof and more accurately recreated mission churches from the Spanish colonial times. San Miguel remains one of the historical wonders of Santa Fe. (Photo by Lail.)

Fig 2.20: San Miguel Mission, c. 1870s. The three-tiered tower structure, built in 1830 by Don Simon Delgado, was destroyed in a wind storm in 1872. (Courtesy of MNM, #66,022 by B. Wittick.)

THE OLD CHURCH SAN MIGUEL
SANTA FE, N.M.

Fig 2.21: San Miguel Mission, 1903. Because of the deterioration of the church seen in the photograph above, San Miguel Mission had to undergo dramatic reconstruction to save the structure. Buttresses and stucco were added to preserve its thick adobe walls. (Courtesy of RGHC-NMSU, Luther Foster Collection, Ms 264.4 by C.G. Kaadt.)

FIG 2.22: SAN MIGUEL MISSION AND ST. MICHAEL'S COLLEGE, 1881. Built by the Christian Brothers in 1878, St. Michael's College (to the right of San Miguel Mission) served as a thriving campus until 1947. The three-story building stood as the largest and tallest adobe structure in Santa Fe, and reflected the French architectural styles introduced by Bishop Lamy. In 1926, the building's mansard roof, tower, and third floor were destroyed by fire. (Courtesy of MNM, #1,403 by W.H. Jackson.)

FIG 2.23: SAN MIGUEL MISSION, 1882. St. Michael's College towers above the mainly one-story adobe structures of territorial Santa Fe. This side view of San Miguel Mission (to the left of the College) show its crenelated parapets, which look more like a Moorish castle. The Santa Fe Trail, crossing the river by the bridge on the left, brought wagons full of traders from the east. Beginning in 1821, these traders caused an economic, cultural, and architectural transformation of New Mexico, shifting the region's alliance away from Mexico and toward the United States. (Courtesy of MNM, #15,230 by W.H. Jackson.)

FIG 2.24: SAN MIGUEL MISSION. The Mission retained the above style until 1955, when a major remodeling and renovation project took place. Artwork, discovered under layers of paint, required hundreds of hours of restoration. The hipped roof and Victorian louvers were replaced with the present-day open bell tower and the flat Pueblo Spanish-style roof. (Courtesy of NMSRAC-DOD, Box 48, #1,477.)

FIG 2.25: SAN MIGUEL MISSION, 1935. Curious visitors from around the world have come to San Miguel Mission to enjoy the architecture and rich history of the oldest church in the United States. This group of visitors was probably only able to see the outside of the church, as it was only open for Sunday Mass. Eventually, the state of New Mexico passed a law requiring that the Mission stay open six days a week. (Courtesy of MNM, #10,107 by T.H. Parkhurst.)

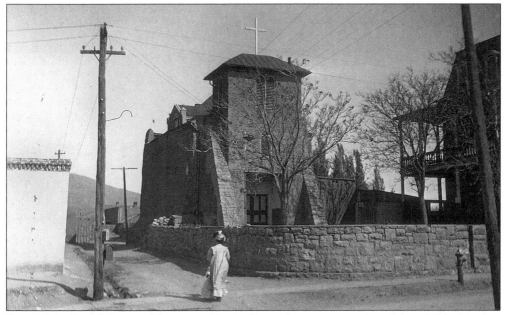

FIG 2.26: SAN MIGUEL MISSION, 1909. Over the centuries, San Miguel Mission has undergone numerous restorations and alterations. In 1887, the buttresses on both sides of the chapel were added to support the massive adobe walls. When compared with the contemporary image below, San Miguel retains its timelessness, despite the cycle of changes. (Courtesy of MNM, #48,338.)

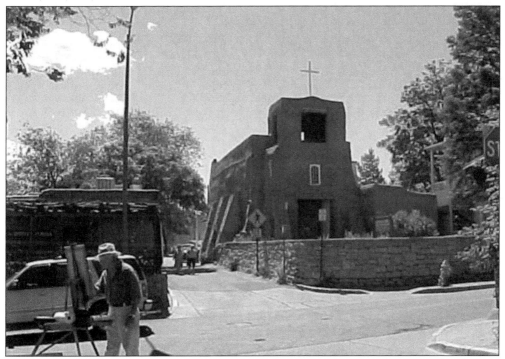

FIG 2.27: SAN MIGUEL MISSION, 2000. Artist Ernesto Zepeda paints a picture of Old Santa Fe Trail, which runs in front of the Mission. (Photo by Lail.)

FIG 2.28: THE OLDEST HOUSE (215 EAST DE VARGAS), 1885. To the north of San Miguel Mission stands the Oldest House. This structure is located in one of Santa Fe's oldest neighborhoods, the Barrio de Analco. Tree ring samples taken from the house's *vigas* date the adobe building to approximately 1740; however, archeological data from the structure's foundation pushes the possible date of occupation back to the late 1300s—before Spanish settlement. (Courtesy of MNM, #14,044 by D.B. Chase.)

FIG 2.29: THE OLDEST HOUSE, 1912. In 1881, Archbishop Lamy purchased the home, along with San Miguel Mission and the property surrounding the Mission, for $3,000. The house was used as an extension to the Mission, where workers could cook meals, sleep, and store supplies for San Miguel. (Courtesy of MNM, #61,429 by J.L. Nusbaum.)

FIG 2.30: THE OLDEST HOUSE. After centuries of wear and tear, the second story of the Oldest House was removed in 1902. For the next several decades, the house remained a single-story adobe. (Courtesy of NMSRAC-DOD, Box 48, #1,565.)

FIG 2.31: THE OLDEST HOUSE. In the mid-1900s, a second story was added to the structure to restore the building's former appearance. Known as one of the oldest houses in the United States, the old adobe attracts many curious tourists. (Courtesy of NMSRAC-DOD, Box 48, #1,452.)

FIG 2.32: THE OLDEST HOUSE, 2000. Like many old buildings in Santa Fe, part of the Oldest House is authentic and part is a recreation. (Photo by Lail.)

Fig 2.33: Barrio de Analco (De Vargas Street), 1879. Indian servants, mainly Tlaxcalans from Mexico who accompanied the first Spanish settlers, established the neighborhood surrounding San Miguel Mission. This neighborhood south of the Plaza was called Barrio de Analco (Analco meaning "other side of the river" in the Nahuatl language of the Tlaxcalans). San Miguel Mission rises on the right. Many Native Americans lived in the Barrio de Analco in the early 1600s, and worked as servants for the Spanish settlers and for the Mission. Eventually, the barrio had a large *mestizo* (mixed heritage) population, which helped to bridge the cultural gap between the early Spanish settlers and the Native American population. (Courtesy of MNM, #15,853 by B. Wittick.)

FIG. 2.34: LA PARROQUIA (131 CATHEDRAL PLACE), 1866. A place of worship has existed on this site since 1626, when Fray Alonso de Benavides built a church here. It was destroyed during the Pueblo Revolt in 1680. The church, called La Parroquia, was rebuilt from 1710 to 1712, and looked like a Moorish castle. The chapel of our Lady of the Rosary formed the northern portion of the transept, and was dedicated to the small 16th century wooden statue of the Virgin known as *La Conquistadora*. The statue, still seen in the cathedral, is one of only two Catholic artifacts that survived the Pueblo Revolt. (Courtesy of MNM, #11,330.)

FIG. 2.35: ST. FRANCIS CATHEDRAL (131 CATHEDRAL PLACE), 1880. In 1869, Archbishop Jean Baptiste Lamy ordered that a French Romanesque Cathedral be built to replace La Parroquia, and the cathedral was completed in 1884. As seen here during construction, the locally quarried stone walls of the cathedral surrounded the old adobe La Parroquia, which remained in use until the structure was completed. (Courtesy of MNM, #131,794 by B.H. Gurnsey.)

FIG. 2.36: EAST SAN FRANCISCO STREET, 1890. Looking east from the Plaza, St. Francis Cathedral dominated the downtown area during the Gilded Age. On the right is the Exchange Hotel. On the wall on the left is a sign for "Albert's," and over the next doorway a sign advertises "Restaurant-Ladies Entrance." (Courtesy of MNM, #15,325 by W.E. Hook.)

FIG. 2.37: ST. FRANCIS CATHEDRAL AND THE SISTERS OF CHARITY'S SCHOOL AND HOSPITAL (CATHEDRAL PLACE), 1887. The completed Sisters of Charity building housed an Industrial School and St. Vincent de Paul's Orphanage and Hospital. Unfortunately, it burned on June 14, 1896. (Courtesy of MNM, #15,167 by Dana B. Chase.)

FIG. 2.38: INDUSTRIAL SCHOOL, 1881. As seen from the north wall of the cathedral during construction, the Sisters of Charity Industrial School for Girls was also a hospital. Both the cathedral and the school utilized the Victorian architectural styles which transformed Santa Fe in the 1880s. (Courtesy of MNM, #15,857 by Ben Wittick.)

FIG. 2.39: ST. VINCENT SANITARIUM, 1893. The Sisters of Charity first opened a hospital in Santa Fe in 1865. The hospital shown here served as an orphanage and a sanitarium. Many people with tuberculosis came to New Mexico for the dry climate that helped cure their disease. (Courtesy of MNM, #67,743.)

FIG. 2.40: STREET SCENE IN SANTA FE, C. 1920S. Looking east down San Francisco Street toward St. Francis Cathedral, one can see how the Ford Model T has replaced burro-drawn wagons in the streets of the "City Different." (Courtesy of NMSRAC-DOD, Box 48, #1,546.)

FIG. 2.41: THE CATHEDRAL, 1900. In the original plans for the cathedral, two huge spires rose to the heavens. When Lamy died in 1888, the momentum for the cathedral's construction also died, and the spires were never completed. (Courtesy of MNM, #13,250 by Rev. John C. Gullette.)

FIG. 2.42: ST. FRANCIS CATHEDRAL, c. 1940S. Santa Feans gathered inside St. Francis Cathedral for the yearly fiesta honoring Don Diego de Vargas's re-conquest of New Mexico in 1692. The Fiesta court is seated on the front pews. (Courtesy of NMSRAC-DOD, Box 15, #47,933.)

Fig. 2.43: St. Francis Cathedral, 1919. Wagons rest in front of St. Francis Cathedral. The adobe buildings across the street from the cathedral (seen in fig. 2.44) were torn down in 1919. (Courtesy of MNM, #13,951 by Wesley Bradfield.)

FIG. 2.44: CATHEDRAL PLACE, 1912. Seen from the intersection of Cathedral Place and Palace Avenue, a row of old adobe residences are seen on the right, and the cathedral is on the left. The adobe buildings once housed the Santa Fe schoolhouse, and later became private homes. (Courtesy of MNM, #61,449 by Jesse L. Nusbaum.)

FIG. 2.45: U.S. POST OFFICE (108 CATHEDRAL PLACE). In 1922, a new post office was built on the site of the old adobe schoolhouse. Designed in the Pueblo Spanish style, the post office helped reinvent Santa Fe's architectural and cultural landscape. (Courtesy of MNM, #56,431.)

FIG. 2.46: EAST SAN FRANCISCO STREET, c. 1940s. Compared to the street scene in fig. 2.36, everything on East San Francisco Street, except the cathedral, has changed to conform to Santa Fe style. (Courtesy of NMSRAC-DOD, Box 48, #1,495.)

FIG. 2.47: EAST SAN FRANCISCO STREET, 2000. The thriving East San Francisco Street, bordered by La Fonda Hotel on the right and businesses on the left, continues to be anchored by St. Francis Cathedral. (Photo by Lail.)

Fig. 2.48: Sena Plaza, 125–137 East Palace Avenue, 1900. The two-story structure on the right is the west wing of the Sena compound, which surrounds Sena Plaza. The land where Sena Plaza now stands was acquired by Arias de Quiros in 1698, when Don Diego de Vargas granted it to him for his participation in the Spanish Re-conquest. Quiros built a two-room house, which no longer exists. The land was later inherited by Maria del Rosario Alarid, wife of Don Juan Sena, in 1844. (Courtesy of MNM, #99,584.)

FIG. 2.49: SENA PLAZA, LOOKING EAST, 1929. Major José D. Sena, who later fought for the Union during the Civil War, inherited the Sena property and began a massive expansion, which eventually included 33 rooms—enough for Sena, his wife, and their 11 children. The family occupied the south, east, and west rooms of the plaza, with the livestock and servants occupying the north rooms. Eventually, Sena added a second story on the west side of his compound. This addition accommodated the Territorial Legislature, which met here after the Territorial Capitol burned in 1892. Also note the 1927 addition of the portal. (Courtesy of MNM, #124,373 by W. Bynner.)

FIG. 2.50: PRINCE AND SENA PLAZA, 2000. Looking east along Palace Avenue from the Plaza, Prince and Sena Plazas are on the left. Sena Plaza begins where the two-story structure is at center right. (Photo by Lail.)

FIG. 2.51: PALACE AVENUE, 1921. A parade of automobiles passes the portal of Prince Plaza. The hitching post in front of the portal was fast becoming obsolete, as cars replaced horses. Even electric power lines were snaking through the "City Different." The automobile ushered in a new period of tourism, which would come to dominate Santa Fe and its environs. (Courtesy of MNM, #150,080 by H. Roberts.)

FIG. 2.52: PALACE AVENUE AT PRINCE PLAZA, 2000. From the portal in front of Prince Plaza, a different parade of vehicles pass by the north side of Old Post Office on Cathedral Place. (Photo by Lail.)

FIG. 2.53: INTERIOR COURTYARD OF SENA PLAZA, 1928–1930. In 1927, artist William Penhallow Henderson began a restoration of Sena Plaza. An oasis of tranquility in the hustle of downtown Santa Fe, the large courtyard of Sena Plaza can be entered at 125 East Palace Avenue. (Courtesy of MNM, #51,558 by T. Harmon Parkhurst.)

FIG. 2.54: SENA PLAZA. Looking west along Palace Avenue from almost the same location as figure 2.48, the addition of the portal to the Sena House is seen. Just to the left of Sena Plaza is Prince Plaza. (Courtesy of NMSRCA, DOD, Box 48, #1,464.)

Gov Princes residence

FIG. 2.55: PRINCE PLAZA (113–115 EAST PALACE AVENUE), 1919. L. Bradford Prince, territorial governor of New Mexico from 1889 to 1893, lived in Prince Plaza, located between the Plaza and Sena Plaza. In 1879, he purchased the building from Carmen Benavides de Robidoux, widow of Antoine Robidoux, an early Santa Fe trader and merchant who arrived in Santa Fe in 1823. Prince later became president of the Historical Society of New Mexico, founded in the 1880s. (Courtesy of MNM, #88,800, by Charles F. Coffin.)

FIG. 2.56: PORTAL AT PRINCE PLAZA, 2000. Shaded by the portal in front of Prince Plaza, a tourist finds refuge from the summer heat. (Photo by Lail.)

FIG. 2.57: 109 EAST PALACE AVENUE, 1958. Through this door passed the greatest scientific minds of the 20th century. During World War II, this door was the gateway to Los Alamos, where the atomic bomb was created. Everyone traveling to Los Alamos was given this address to direct them, unaware that a 40-mile trip to the top secret community still awaited them. (Courtesy of MNM, #91,931 by Tyler Dingee.)

Three

NORTH, WEST, AND
SOUTHWEST OF THE PLAZA

FIG. 3.1: SANTA FE FROM FORT MARCY HILL, 1866. Looking south from Fort Marcy Hill, La Parroquia rises above the cornfield in the center of the photo. The Plaza is behind the buildings on the right. When the United States conquered New Mexico in 1846, the U.S. Army built Fort Marcy on this hill above the town. After the Treaty of Guadalupe-Hidalgo, the army relocated its fort downtown. Fort Marcy then included the Palace of the Governors and the presidio which occupied all of the area from the Plaza north to the where the Federal Courthouse now stands. (Courtesy of MNM, #38,176.)

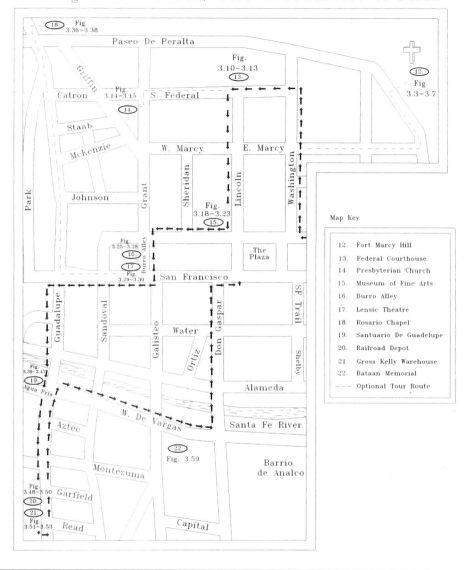

FIG. 3.2: MAP OF THE AREA NORTH, WEST, AND SOUTHWEST OF THE PLAZA. Several sites might be too far to walk, so those are listed as optional tour routes.

FIG. 3.3: SANTA FE FROM FORT MARCY HILL, c. 1890s. Looking west from Fort Marcy Hill, one sees how Santa Fe grew dramatically in the last half of the 19th century. The tall building in the center with the dark roof is the Palace Hotel. The building to the right with the triangular roof is the Federal Courthouse. As the U.S. Army moved into the presidio left by the Mexican Army, they built new facilities for their men, livestock, equipment, and traditions. The flagpole seen here between the Palace Hotel and the Courthouse rises above Fort Marcy's parade grounds. (Courtesy of RGHC-NMSU, Blazer Collection, Ms. 110-7.3.4 by Dana B. Chase.)

FIG. 3.4: SANTA FE FROM FORT MARCY HILL, 2000. As seen from Fort Marcy Hill, downtown Santa Fe is now packed with buildings and trees. The cross commemorates the Franciscan martyrs killed in the Pueblo Revolt. The walkway up to the cross from Paseo de Peralta is lined with bronze plaques, which recount the history of the Santa Fe. (Photo by Lail.)

FIG. 3.5: SANTA FE FROM FORT MARCY HILL, 2000. Looking south from Fort Marcy Hill, the unfinished towers of St. Francis Cathedral are visible to the left of the radio tower. To the right of the radio tower, the spire of the Bataan Building, a state governmental office building, rises above the horizon. The Bataan Building resides on the site of the Old State Capitol. (see figs. 3.56 and 3.59). (Photo by Lail.)

FIG. 3.6: ZOZOBRA (SANTA FE'S SPORTS COMPLEX, 490 WASHINGTON AVENUE), 1947. In 1926, artists Will Shuster and Gustave Baumann created Zozobra as part of the fiesta that commemorates the re-conquest of Santa Fe in 1692. On Friday night at the start of the Fiesta, Santa Feans transfer all their cares and worries to Zozobra (also known as "Old Man Gloom"). As they chant "burn him," he goes up in flames and celebrants enter the spirit of Fiesta with a carefree and merry heart. (Courtesy of MNM, #41,301 by Robert Martin.)

FIG. 3.7: SANTA FE FROM FORT MARCY HILL, 1904. Looking south from Fort Marcy Hill in 1904, the prominent buildings exhibit ornate architectural details unknown to Santa Fe before the railroad arrived. On the left, St. Vincent's Hospital, the County Courthouse, and the Old State Capitol show how far Santa Feans moved away from their Native American, Spanish, and

Mexican architectural roots in constructing their city. On the right is the Palace Hotel. As the new architectural styles transformed the public and private buildings of Santa Fe, places like the Palace Hotel supplanted the Exchange Hotel as one of the premier lodging establishments in town. (Courtesy of MNM, #10,173.)

FIG. 3.8: PALACE HOTEL (125 WASHINGTON STREET), 1880–1883. The Palace Hotel illustrates the changing look of the "City Different" during the late 1800s. With its Second Empire architectural style, the Palace Hotel reveled in its mansard roof and decorative wrought-iron railings. Many of the buildings constructed after the railroad arrived in 1881 used new building materials and reflected East Coast and northern European architectural styles. (Courtesy of MNM, #10,766.)

FIG. 3.9: PALACE HOTEL, 1922. This drawing shows how the Palace Hotel would have looked after having been remodeled in the Pueblo Spanish style. While being remodeled in January 1922, the Palace Hotel burned to the ground. Many Victorian buildings in Santa Fe were remodeled after 1910 to conform to the Pueblo Spanish style. (Courtesy of MNM, #61,428 by Jesse L. Nusbaum.)

FIG. 3.10: FEDERAL BUILDING, 1890–1891. Begun in the 1850s, the Federal Building remained unfinished until 1889. By then, the state capitol building was completed across town, and so the Court of Private Lands Claims and the U.S. Land Office set up shop in the building. For an 1883 celebration commemorating the founding of Santa Fe, a racetrack for horse and burro racing circled the grounds. The oval street that today curves around the courthouse and post office next door are remnants of the racetrack. (Courtesy of MNM, #56,983.)

FIG. 3.11: FEDERAL COURTHOUSE, 2000. Except for the trees and nearby buildings, the Federal Courthouse has changed little since its completion in 1889. (Photo by Lail.)

FIG. 3.12: FEDERAL BUILDING, 1888. Looking south from the Federal Building, Fort Marcy flanked both sides of Lincoln Avenue. The Plaza, under the clump of trees center left, and the newly built State Capitol with its domed rotunda (center left) could be seen from the top windows of the building. The flagpole on the right anchored the parade ground at Fort Marcy. (Courtesy of MNM, #105,946.)

FIG. 3.13: FEDERAL COURTHOUSE, 2000. The U.S. District Court resides in the building today. The obelisk on the left was erected in 1885 in memory of Kit Carson—explorer, Civil War and Indian War veteran, and military scout—who died on May 23, 1868. (Photo by Lail.)

FIG. 3.14: PRESBYTERIAN CHURCH, c. 1879–1881. In 1854, along with the introduction from the United States of distinctive customs and practices, came a new religion to the region. The Baptists built one of the first Protestant churches in New Mexico at the corner of Grant and Griffin Streets. Constructed of adobe, it was purchased by the Presbyterians in 1867. William Bonney (aka Billy the Kid) attended his mother's marriage ceremony to William Antrim on March 1, 1873, in this church. (Courtesy of MNM, #15,855.)

FIG. 3.15: PRESBYTERIAN CHURCH, 1912. In 1912, the Presbyterians remodeled their church into a Gothic Revival brick structure with arched windows and a bell tower. As often happened in Santa Fe, the church was transformed into a Pueblo Spanish style structure in 1939. (Courtesy of MNM, #15,175.)

Fig. 3.16: San Esteban del Rey Mission and Convent (Pueblo of Acoma), 1935. The Mission at the Pueblo of Acoma was originally built in 1629. Its design inspired the Pueblo Spanish architectural movement in Santa Fe in the 1910s and 1920s. The Pueblo Spanish style swept through Santa Fe during this period, and helped Santa Fe recreate itself as a Spanish colonial town and the "City Different." (Courtesy of MNM, #7,864.)

Fig. 3.17: New Mexico Building at the Panama-California Exposition (San Diego, California), 1915. The New Mexico Building, shown here under construction, housed an exhibit of New Mexican arts and culture at the Panama-California Exposition in San Diego in 1916. The architectural firm of Rapp, Rapp, and Hendrickson designed the building based on the San Esteban del Rey Mission and Convent at the Pueblo of Acoma. (Courtesy of MNM, #60,254.)

FIG. 3.18: MUSEUM OF FINE ARTS (107 WEST PALACE AVENUE), c. 1920. Built in 1917, the museum was constructed using the blueprints from the New Mexico Building at the Panama-California Exposition seen in figure 3.17. The appearance of a Native American pueblo in downtown Santa Fe helped revolutionize the look of the "City Different," and a unique architectural genre, the Pueblo Spanish style, was created. (Courtesy of MNM, #22,968.)

FIG. 3.19: MUSEUM OF FINE ARTS, 2000. On the northwest corner of the Plaza, the Museum of Fine Arts continues to be an architectural icon. (Photo by Lail.)

Fig. 3.20: Museum of Fine Arts, 1941. As in figure 3.19, crowds await the Fiesta parade in front of the museum. (Courtesy of NMSRAC-DOD, Box 15, #47,888.)

FIG. 3.21: MUSEUM OF FINE ARTS. The Palace on the right and the Museum of Fine Arts in the center led the way in creating the Pueblo Spanish style, a new regional architectural style. (Courtesy of NMSRAC-DOD, Box 48, #1,535.)

FIG. 3.22: COURTYARD OF THE MUSEUM OF FINE ARTS, c. 1920S. Native Americans from the Pueblo of Tesuque demonstrate one of their ceremonial dances. Notice that the audience is composed mainly of women. (Courtesy of RGHC, Foster Collection, Ms 264.32.)

FIG. 3.23: COURTYARD OF THE MUSEUM OF FINE ARTS, c. 1920S. Native Americans from the Pueblo of Santa Clara perform a dance in the museum's courtyard. The headdresses are not from pueblo culture, but are typical of Plains Indians. Many pueblos near Santa Fe perform Comanche War dances in tribute to their ancestral enemies. (Courtesy of RGHC-NMSU, Foster Collection, Ms 264.33.)

FIG. 3.24: HEWETT HOUSE (118 LINCOLN AVENUE), 1918. In 1868, officers' quarters were built at this site by the U.S. Army as part of Fort Marcy. The Hewett House, seen here with a flag in front, is one of the few surviving structures from Fort Marcy. The brick house on the right shows the original style. After remodeling, Edgar Hewett, the director of the Museum of Fine Arts, moved into the home. Hewett was one of the key promoters of the Pueblo Spanish style and helped reinvent Santa Fe. (Courtesy of MNM, #28,862.)

FIG. 3.25: BURRO ALLEY (EAST OF 211 WEST SAN FRANCISCO STREET), c. 1880–1885.
Burro Alley lies between West San Francisco Street and West Palace Avenue. During the 19th century, Burro Alley was the place where residents could leave their burros, get a drink of "Taos Lightning" whiskey, and gamble at three-card monte. The largest of the gambling houses in Burro Alley was run by Doña Tules Barcello. The Santa Fe Courthouse now stands where her saloon once did. (Courtesy of MNM, #51,700.)

Fig. 3.26: Burro Alley, c. 1895–1898. The street light on the left (gaslights were installed in 1881) no longer has its glass lamp, possibly due to the effects of the Taos Lightning sold nearby. The shop on the left has a caretta on top of the roof to get the attention of potential customers. The shop sold items such as Indian pottery. (Courtesy of MNM, #11,070 by C.G. Kaadt.)

FIG. 3.27: BURRO ALLEY, 1900. Santa Feans used the burro as the beast of burden for over three centuries. The burros carried firewood down from the mountains, which was then sold at Burro Alley. The Curiosity Shop at right is one of the oldest tourist shops in Santa Fe. (Courtesy of MNM, #87,028 by Royal Hubbell.)

FIG. 3.28: BURRO ALLEY, 2000. Cafes and boutiques have replaced saloons and gambling houses at Burro Alley. The Lensic Theater is on the left side of the Burro Alley. (Courtesy of Lail.)

FIG. 3.29: LENSIC THEATER (211 WEST SAN FRANCISCO STREET), 1937. Opened in June 1931 as a vaudeville and motion picture house, the Lensic Theater was known as the "wonder theater of the southwest" with its unusual Moorish-Spanish-style architecture. Built by Nathan Salmon and E. John Greer, it received its name from the first letter of each of Salmon's six grandchildren. Such entertainers as Rudy Vallee, Rita Hayworth, Claudette Colbert, Johnny Weismuller, Roy Rogers, Errol Flynn, Ronald Reagan, and Judy Garland performed at the Lensic. (Courtesy of MNM, #51,556 by T. Harmon Parkhurst.)

FIG. 3.30: LENSIC THEATER, 2000. As of this writing, the Lensic Theater was closed for a major renovation. After the construction is completed, the Lensic will serve as a performance space for many of the cultural institutions in Santa Fe. (Photo by Lail.)

FIG. 3.31: CROSS OF THE MARTYRS, 1920. The Cross of the Martyrs on Rosario Hill is seen here under construction. The cross commemorates the 21 Franciscans martyred during the Pueblo Revolt of 1680. The cross is 25 feet high and weighs 76 tons. To get to the cross, take Paseo de Peralta and turn on Paseo de la Cuma and then right onto Paseo de la Loma. The cross is up the hill on Paseo de la Loma. (Courtesy of MNM, #57,998.)

Fig. 3.32: The Dedication of the Cross of the Martyrs, 1920. As part of the Fiesta de Santa Fe of 1920, the Cross of the Martyrs was dedicated on September 15. Notice the variety of celebrants, including the Boy Scouts in the center from Los Alamos (when it was a boys' school). The plaque on the base reads: "Erected by the Knights of Columbus and the Historical Society of New Mexico in memory of the Franciscan Friars who were killed by the Pueblo Indians in the revolution in the province of New Mexico August 9 and 10, A.D. 1680." (Courtesy of MNM, #52,462 by H.C. Tibbits.)

FIG. 3.33: VIEW FROM THE CROSS OF THE MARTYRS. Looking east from Rosario Hill, downtown Santa Fe looks distant and shows how Rosario Hill was isolated in the 1920s. Now residences surround the cross. (Courtesy of MNM, #52,463.)

FIG. 3.34: CROSS OF THE MARTYRS. In this promotional photograph, a man dressed as a Spanish Conquistador is surrounded by children representing the three cultures of Santa Fe. (Courtesy of NMSRAC-DOD, Box 48, #1,496.)

Fig. 3.35: Hayt-Wientge House (620 Paseo de la Cuma), 1890. Walter Hayt built this Victorian home on Rosario Hill in 1882. As compared to the adobe house in the foreground, the new architectural style of homes like the Hayt-Wientge House during the late 1800s altered the look of Santa Fe. (Courtesy of MNM, #89,281 by Dana Chase.)

Fig. 3.36: Rosario Chapel (in the Rosario Cemetery at the corner of Paseo de Peralta and Guadalupe Street), 1911. Rosario Chapel, built in 1807, provides the staging ground for the de Vargas Pageant in 1911. Four pueblo governors accompany George Armijo, who plays Don Diego de Vargas. (Courtesy of MNM, #117,756 by Jesse L. Nusbaum.)

FIG. 3.37: ROSARIO CHAPEL, 1933. Once a year during Fiesta, Rosario Chapel hosts La Conquistadora, a sacred statue brought from St. Francis Cathedral. The Fiesta, an annual celebration of Don Diego de Vargas's re-conquest of New Mexico, consists of both religious and secular events. (Courtesy of MNM, #55,478 by Mack.)

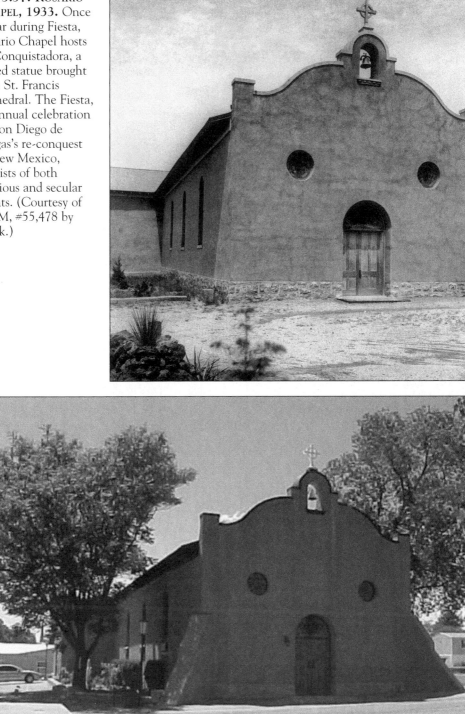

FIG. 3.38: ROSARIO CHAPEL, 2000. Corner buttresses have been added to brace the adobe walls of the chapel. (Photo by Lail.)

111

FIG. 3.39: SANTUARIO DE GUADALUPE (100 SOUTH GUADALUPE STREET), 1882. The Santuario de Guadalupe Church was built in the late 1700s, and served one of oldest neighborhoods of colonial Santa Fe. The Camino Real, the Royal Road which connected Santa Fe to Mexico City for 250 years, passed by the Santuario de Guadalupe, and many travelers stopped and gave thanks at the altar before they entered the town. The altar painting, brought up the Camino Real from Mexico City in 1783, remains in the Santuario and shines as a jewel of Spanish colonial devotional art. (Courtesy of MNM, #132,561 by W.H. Jackson.)

FIG. 3.40: SANTUARIO DE GUADALUPE. After Bishop Lamy took over the diocese, he altered the look of the Catholic churches in Santa Fe. The Santuario de Guadalupe acquired a steeple, a pitched roof, and arched windows. (Courtesy of MNM, #15,145 by F.A. Nims.)

FIG. 3.41: SANTUARIO DE GUADALUPE. After a fire in 1922, Lamy's alteration of the Santuario gave way to the California Mission style. The tracks of the Denver and Rio Grande Railroad, which ran from Santa Fe to Denver, cross in front of the church. (Courtesy of MNM, #15,143.)

FIG. 3.42: SANTUARIO DE GUADALUPE, 1928. The Santuario has been a center of community activity for centuries. In 1961, a new church opened to the west of the colonial structure. (Courtesy of MNM, # 10,038 by T.Harmon Parkhurst.)

FIG. 3.43: SANTUARIO DE GUADALUPE, 2000. In 1976, the old Santuario was restored to a Pueblo Spanish-style building and is now a cultural center. The 1976 restoration brought the look of the Santuario back full circle, to how it might have looked in the early 1800s. (Photo by Lail.)

FIG. 3.44: SANTUARIO DE GUADALUPE. Looking west over rooftops, the Santuario rises on the right above the neighborhood. (Courtesy NMSRAC-DOD, Box 52, #2,183.)

FIG. 3.45: SANTUARIO DE GUADALUPE, 2000. With square openings in the tower and over the doors, the Santuario lost some of the California Mission look with the 1976 restoration. (Photo by Lail.)

FIG. 3.46: SANTUARIO DE GUADALUPE, 1941. The Denver and Rio Grande Railroad ran in front of the Santuario de Guadalupe. The last run of the D&RG Railroad passed the Santuario on its way north on September 1, 1941. This narrow gauge railroad, also known as the "Chile Line," hauled freight and passengers from Santa Fe and northern New Mexico to Colorado and Denver. (Courtesy of MNM, #41,833 by Margaret McKittrick.)

FIG. 3.47: SANTUARIO DE GUADALUPE, 2000. Looking from the same angle as figure 3.46, the landscape around the Santuario has changed some since the railroad ran along Guadalupe Street, but little else has changed. (Photo by Lail.)

FIG. 3.48: RAILROAD DEPOT (500 SOUTH GUADALUPE STREET), 1929. The arrival of the Atchison, Topeka, & Santa Fe Railroad into Santa Fe in February of 1880 forever changed Santa Fe. Not only did the railroad open greater markets for goods and make it easier to move products to and from the city, but the railroad also brought with it a burgeoning tourism industry and new architectural styles. Notice the proper, well-dressed travelers waiting for the train, and the horse-drawn carriages and wagons ready to move goods nearby. (Courtesy of MNM, #66,658 by Jesse L. Nusbaum.)

FIG. 3.49: RAILROAD DEPOT, 2000. Pickup trucks have replaced horse-drawn wagons as the beasts of burden in modern Santa Fe. (Photo by Lail.)

FIG. 3.50: RAILROAD DEPOT, 2000. A tourist train now runs daily from the depot to Lamy, 20 miles south of the town. In actuality, the Atchison, Topeka, and Santa Fe Railroad never ran a mainline through its namesake. A spur line was built in the 1880s over the rolling hills from Lamy to Santa Fe, to connect the town with the AT&SF. (Photo by Lail.)

119

**FIG. 3.51: GROSS, KELLY, AND COMPANY WAREHOUSE (430 WEST MANHATTAN STREET),
1920.** The Gross, Kelly, and Company warehouse at the rail yard was the first commercial
structure in Santa Fe built in the Pueblo Spanish style. Designed by architect Isaac Hamilton
Rapp in 1913, the design of the structure was modeled after the Pecos Pueblo and mission
church, which later became the Pecos National Monument. (Courtesy of MNM, #10,710 by
Wesley Bradfield.)

FIG. 3.52: VIEW FROM THE OLD STATE CAPITOL, 1916. This photo and figure 3.54 are
companion views of the city, looking to the northeast from the roof of the Old State Capitol.
The Governor's Mansion is on the left. The twin stacks of the city's power plant are center with
the Palace Hotel just to the right of the smokestacks. St. Francis Cathedral can clearly be seen
at center right. (Courtesy of MNM, #10,144.)

FIG. 3.53: GROSS, KELLY, AND COMPANY WAREHOUSE, 2000. Now the warehouse provides space for tourist stores, artist studios, and a performance space. It still looks remarkably similar to its original appearance. (Photo by Lail.)

FIG. 3.54: VIEW FROM THE OLD STATE CAPITOL, 1916. Loretto Chapel and St. Michael's College are seen on the left, with the Santa Fe River running through the center of the photo. (Courtesy of MNM, #10,148.)

FIG. 3.55: NEW MEXICO TERRITORIAL CAPITOL, 1890. The first two New Mexico Territorial Capitol buildings no longer exist. After heated debates over which town would become the capital, with Albuquerque attempting to secure the honor, Santa Fe won—and erected this building in 1885. A twin-domed structure, it burned down in 1892, possibly due to arson, although this was never proved. (Courtesy of RGHC-NMSU, #A76-157/166.)

FIG. 3.56: NEW MEXICO STATE CAPITOL, 1900. A new Territorial Capitol became the state capitol building in 1912. This single-domed building was erected in 1900 to replace the previous capitol, which burned in 1892. With its Greek Revival style, the building did not fit with the Pueblo Spanish style, which came to dominate Santa Fe architecture after the 1910s. (Courtesy of RGHC-NMSU, Ms. 264.31 by Luther Foster.)

122

Fig. 3.57: Capitol Building, May 5, 1903. In 1903, nine years before statehood, President Theodore Roosevelt visited Santa Fe and spoke to a crowd of over ten thousand. The president arrived at nine in the morning to a 21-gun salute, and made his way to the capitol steps, where he was introduced by Governor Otero. After thanking New Mexicans for serving as his "Rough Riders" during the Spanish-American War, Roosevelt declared that as president he would represent New Mexico no less than any other part of the nation. (Courtesy of MNM, #8,111 by E. Andrews.)

FIG. 3.58: STATE CAPITOL, 1950. The end of an era arrived in 1950 for the Old State Capitol building as the temple-front entry, where President Theodore Roosevelt once stood, was dismantled, and the rest of the building was remodeled. The dome was removed, and the entire structure was drastically renovated to look like a Territorial-style building to harmonize with Santa Fe style. The former State Capitol is now the Bataan Memorial building. (Courtesy of NMSRAC-DOD, Box 58, #2,895.)

FIG. 3.59: BATAAN BUILDING, 2000. A Territorial-style tower replaced the domed rotunda of the Old State Capitol Building. Still housing state government offices, the Bataan Building commemorates the New Mexicans who served in World War II, especially those who were captured in the Philippines and suffered during the Bataan Death March and imprisonment. (Photo by Lail.)

FIG. 3.60: GOVERNOR'S MANSION, PRE-1955. This structure was built between 1907 and 1909, and served as the residence of the governor of New Mexico until 1950. In 1955, it was torn down as the old capitol was renovated. The present Territorial-style governor's residence is in the hills north of downtown. (Courtesy of NMSRAC-DOD, Box 58, #2,885.)

FIG. 3.61: WITTER BYNNER HOUSE (342 EAST BUENA VISTA), c. 1910s. When the poet Witter Bynner arrived in Santa Fe in 1919, he purchased this aged adobe structure at the corner of Old Santa Fe Trail and Buena Vista Street. (Courtesy of RGHC-NMSU, Bynner Collection, Ms 186.1998.)

FIG. 3.62: WITTER BYNNER HOUSE, c. 1930s. After extensive renovation in the 1920s, the Witter Bynner House not only gained a new lease on life, but also reflected the burgeoning Santa Fe style. Many celebrities, including D.H. and Frieda Lawrence, and Leon Trotsky enjoyed Bynner's famous hospitality. (Courtesy of RGHC, Bynner Collection, Ms 186.1437.)

126

FIG. 3.63: DON GASPAR STREET, 1927. Looking north on Don Gaspar Street, one sees the many businesses that catered to automobiles in the 1920s. The De Vargas Hotel, now Hotel St. Francis, is on the left up the block. At the end of Don Gaspar Street, where it meets West San Francisco Street, is a white building, the Commercial Hotel. To its immediate right is the brick building on the west side of the Plaza (see figure 1.43). (Courtesy of MNM, #51,491.)

REFERENCES

Bullock, Alice. *Loretto and the Miraculous Staircase*. Santa Fe: The Sunstone Press, 1978.

Chaurenet, Beatrice. *John Gaw Meem, Pioneer in Historic Preservation*. Santa Fe: Museum of New Mexico Press, 1985.

Historic Santa Fe Foundation. *Old Santa Fe Today: Third Edition*. Albuquerque: University of New Mexico Press, 1982.

Horgan, Paul. *The Centuries of Santa Fe*. New York: E.P. Dutton and Co. Inc., 1956.

Jamison, Bill. *Insiders Guide to Santa Fe*. Boston: The Harvard Common Press, 1987.
Santa Fe An Intimate View. Santa Fe: Milagro Press, 1982.

Johnson and Nestor. *San Miguel Chapel: Historic Structure Report and Master Plan*. Santa Fe: Johnson-Nestor Architects-Planners, 1978.

Knaut, Andrew. *The Pueblo Revolt: Conquest and Resistance in Seventeenth-Century New Mexico*. Norman: University of Oklahoma Press, 1995.

Kochendoerfer, Violet. *Santa Fe in the Fifties*. Santa Fe: Western Edge Press, 1998.

Kubler, George. *The Rebuilding of San Miguel at Santa Fe in 1710*. Colorado Springs: Taylor Museum of Fine Arts, 1939.

Lafarge, Oliver. *Santa Fe, Autobiography of a Southwestern Town*. Norman: University of Oklahoma Press, 1959.

Mather, Christine and Sharon Woods. *Santa Fe Style*. New York: Rizzoli International Publications, 1986.

Morand, Sheila. *Santa Fe Then and Now*. Santa Fe: Sunstone Press, 1998.

Noble, David G. *Santa Fe: History of an Ancient City*. Santa Fe: School of American Research Press, 1989.

Nusbaum, Rosemary. *The City Different and the Palace, The Palace of the Governors: Its Role in Santa Fe History*. Santa Fe: Sunstone Press, 1978.

Parent, Lawrence. *Sights and Scenes of New Mexico: Santa Fe*. Houston: Gulf Publishing Company, 1996.

Pinkerton, Elaine. *Santa Fe On Foot*. Santa Fe: Ocean Tree Services, 1986.

Sherman, John. *Santa Fe: A Pictorial History*. Norfolk: Donning Company Publishers, 1983.

Simmons, Marc. *New Mexico: An Interpretive History*. Albuquerque: University of New Mexico Press, 1998.
Yesterday in Santa Fe: Episodes in a Turbulent History. Santa Fe: Sunstone Press, 1989.

Thompson, Waite and Richard Gottlieb. *The Santa Fe Guide*. Santa Fe: Sunstone Press, 1993.

Twitchell, Ralph E. *Old Santa Fe: The Story of New Mexico's Ancient Capital*. Chicago: The Rio Grande Press, 1963.

Wilson, Chris. *The Myth of Santa Fe: Creating a Modern Regional Tradition*. Albuquerque: University of New Mexico Press, 1997.